Introduction

This gentle and colourful book is a first introduction to Allah for babies, toddlers, and preschoolers. Through simple words and warm illustrations, children will learn that Allah is One, Kind, Loving, and always near.

Perfect for little hands and growing hearts, this book helps nurture faith, gratitude, and love for our Creator—right from the start.

Who is Allah ?

Allah is the One who made everything! He made the sun, the moon, the stars, the trees, and you and me.

Allah is One

We believe in only one Allah. There is no one like Him. He is always with us, even though we can't see Him.

Allah is Kind

Allah loves us so much. He gives us food to eat, water to drink, and people who care for us.

Allah Hears Us

When we talk to Allah in our duas (prayers), He listens. We can talk to Him any time, about anything.

Allah Sees Us

Allah sees us when we do good things—like sharing toys or helping someone. He is happy when we are kind and loving.

Allah Made Me Special

Allah made every child special and unique. He gave us eyes to see, hands to help, and heart to love.

I Love Allah

We love Allah because He made us, cares for us, and listens to us always.

Let's Thank Allah

Thank You, Allah, for everything!
For love, light, food, and family.
Alhamdulillah!

Point & Count

Point & Count the things in this page that Allah made.
Say their names out loud!

Lets practice Dua

Repeat this short dua with your child

"Thank You Allah, for my day. Help me be good in every way."

Lets learn some arabic words and use them everyday

الله

1. Allah (الله) – God
2. Bismillah (بِسْمِ الله) – In the name of Allah
3. Alhamdulillah (اَلْحَمْدُ لله) – All praise is for Allah
4. Salam (سلام) – Peace
5. Du'a (دُعَاء) – Prayer or asking Allah

Quiz time

Who made you ?	**ALLAH**
What do we say before eating ?	**BISMILLAH**
Where is Allah ?	**EVERYWHERE**
What is the name of our holy book ?	**QURAN**
What do we say when we are happy ?	**ALHUMDULILLAH**

My Dua Card

Draw or Paste a Picture of What
You Want to Ask Allah For!

Dear Allah ,

Today i am grateful for :

Allah mde sun, moon, stars and trees

Can you add some colour ?

Allah made all the animals and birds

Can you add some colour ?

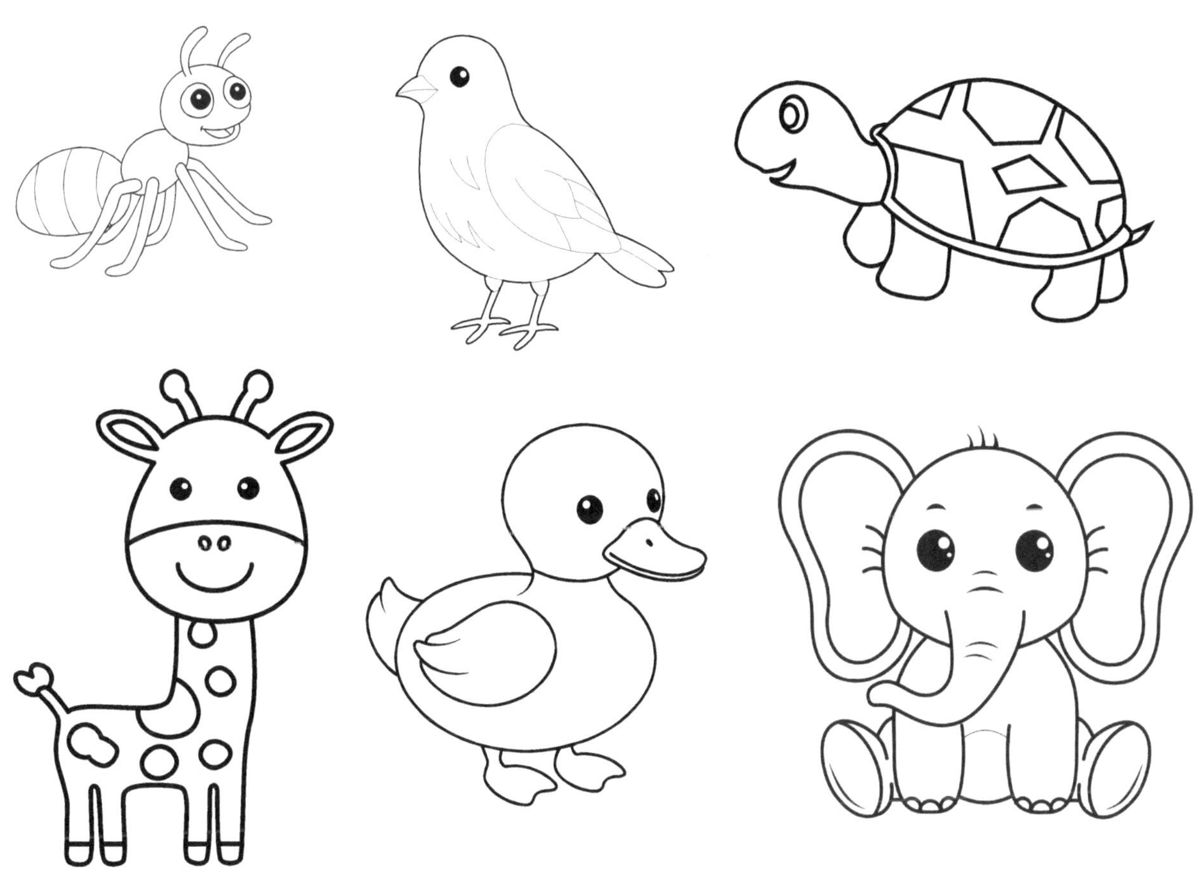

Draw something that you love